Tackling, Contact, Teamwor... ...ics

Contents

When using this book, concentrate on one coaching point at a time. Practise
each point until you have mastered it before moving on to the next one.
You do not need to work through the book from cover to cover. Choose a skill
you want to work on and practise it until you are happy with the outcome.

INTRODUCTION

Welcome to *Tackling, Contact, Teamwork, Tactics*. Rugby is a contact sport and in this book we will be looking at how to prepare yourself to manage contact without losing the ball or hurting yourself. You will also learn how to stop opposition players by tackling them – this is great fun, but you need to know what you are doing!

Rugby players need to work together as a team to beat the opposition. How do you out-think them? You need to use tactics so that you can plan to do what the opposition is least expecting. Like a general in battle, you are trying to out-fox the enemy. The difference is that after the battle we shake hands with the opposition!

DID YOU KNOW?

The game of rugby was invented in 1823 at Rugby school in Warwickshire when a boy named William Webb Ellis picked up the ball and ran with it. It is now played all over the world, and is particularly big in the Southern Hemisphere countries of Australia, New Zealand and South Africa.

In *Passing, Catching, Kicking* we looked at ways of scoring points by kicking penalties, conversions and drop goals. But rugby is essentially a running game and the main objective is to score a try by placing the ball on the ground over the opposition's try line.

You need to practise scoring a try. If you don't, you might drop the ball over the line (instead of placing it on the ground with downwards pressure), in which case all your hard work would be undone as the 'try' would be disallowed.

Here is a first simple practice for scoring a try.

 Rugby is a contact sport and you need to learn how to tackle correctly.

SCORING A TRY

Key points
- Run with the ball in two hands.
- As you cross an imaginary or real line, score a try by firmly placing the ball on the ground.

Make it harder
- Run on after you have put the ball down, leaving it on the ground. Look back – is it lying still on the ground in the same spot? In that case you have grounded it with downward pressure without dropping it and a try is scored. If it is moving, or has moved from the spot where you 'scored' it will not be given as a try and will instead be ruled as a 'knock on'. The opposing team is then given the ball.
- If the ground is soft enough and you don't mind getting muddy, see if you can dive on the ground over the line with the ball held in two hands into your chest.
- Go slowly, putting your knees on the ground first and then dropping down to the floor with your chest.
- Make sure the ball doesn't spill or get knocked out of your hands.
- Don't hold the ball into your tummy, or you may get the wind knocked out of you as you land on it!

 Scoring a try is the object of the game.

AVOIDING A **TACKLE**

You need to learn how to avoid being tackled as you run with the ball. If a defender tries to tackle you and there is no supporting player to pass to, you will need to use your own skills to get past the opposing player. There are a number of ways to beat a defender:

• Run around him. Be so quick that he can't catch you.
• Side-step him. Leave him tackling thin air!
• Swerve around him. Again, leave him trying to tackle the space that you have just run out of.
• Kick the ball past him. Then get it back before he can turn and get it himself.

RUN AROUND

If you can see that you have a slower player in front of you, don't be afraid to have a go at running around him.

Be careful that you don't run away from supporting players and end up getting tackled or running into touch (i.e. running off the pitch, causing the ball to be given to the other team)! Your teammates may be a little disappointed that you didn't pass to them, so the trick is to have a go, and if you see that you are not going to make it, slow up and look for support.

Defender

Player with ball

Avoid tackling by running around the opposing player.

THE SIDE-STEP

The side-step is used to fool the defender into trying to tackle the space he thought you were going to run into.

Key points
• Run towards the defender's inside shoulder – this is the left

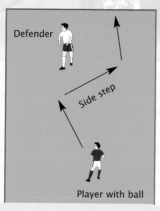

Defender

Side step

Player with ball

Practise avoiding a tackle by using the side-step.

1

2

3

shoulder if you are going to pass them on the right.
- Take short steps as you get near to the defender to help you get your timing and balance right.
- Change direction close to the defender by pushing sideways powerfully off the right foot to go left or the left foot to go right. In the diagram the ball carrier pushes off his left foot to go right.
- Think of your shoulders as the signal that fools the defender. Face them towards the way you want him to think you are going, but as you push off your front foot, turn them to face the new direction.
- You have to be quick to accelerate away while the defender is wrong-footed.

The side-step: 1. Run towards the defender, aiming for the side opposite the one you intend to pass him on.
2. Pretend to run to this side.
3. At the last second, quickly change direction and run round the opposite side.

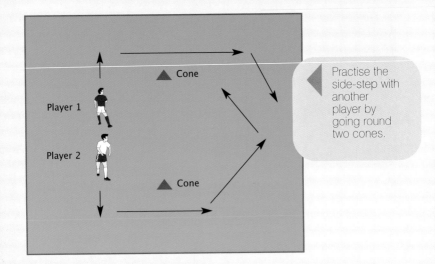

Player 1

Player 2

Cone

Cone

Practise the side-step with another player by going round two cones.

Practice

You will need:
- Just you to start with.
- A rugby ball.
- A marker on the ground to take the place of a defender.

Run up to the mark on the ground and follow the key points described on page 5.

Make it harder

- Ask a partner to join you and take turns being the defender.
- At first, the defender should stand still. Then you can make it more interesting by getting the defender to run as well.
- Use cones or jumpers as markers to run around.

THE SWERVE

The swerve is used to fool the defender into tackling the space he thought you were going to run into, just like the side-step. The difference is that you pivot or swing on one foot to fool the defender. It is most effective combined with a dummy pass.

Key points

- Run towards the defender's inside shoulder. This is the left shoulder if you are going to pass him to the right.
- Take short steps as you get near to the defender to help you get your timing and balance right.

- Change direction close to him by making a pass with your arms towards your supporting player. Then, just as you should let go of the ball, hold on to it and swing around your planted foot to run inside the defender.

BE THE BEST

Practise pivoting on your foot and then sprinting away. You have to be quick to accelerate away while the defender is wrong-footed.

The swerve: 1. Run towards the defender, aiming for the opposite side to the one you intend to go past him on. Just in front of the defender, pretend to make a pass to a supporting player.

2. Quickly pivot on your foot and turn in the opposite direction.

2. Accelerate away while the defender is wrong-footed.

3. Accelerate away while the defender is wrong-footed.

TACKLING

The game of rugby is a contact game. This means that you will have to be good at physically stopping the opposing players by tackling them. The idea of the tackle is not just to stop the opposition player, but also to win the ball back.

It is essential that you only start practising the tackle after you have been coached in the basic techniques by a qualified coach.

Use these ideas to improve your technique away from team practices, but you should have an adult with you when you practise tackling.

BEING TACKLED

This is an important aspect of rugby to get right, as all players will be tackled during a game, and if you lose the ball you won't be very popular with your teammates! We will examine taking the ball into contact later in this book. For now, let's look at how, when you are tackled, you protect yourself and make sure the ball stays with your team.

FALLING IN THE TACKLE

When you are tackled and you are falling to the ground, the main thing to remember is not to put your hand out to stop your

fall, which can lead to injury to your wrist, shoulder or arm. The best way to stop yourself from doing this is to hold the ball in two hands. As you fall, you should roll on to your hip and then your shoulder to break the fall, while you continue to hold the ball in both hands.

Key points

- As the tackler approaches you, try to keep low so that you are harder to tackle.
- Make sure you are holding the ball in both hands.
- Hold the ball away from the tackler by turning towards your own teammates (see more on page 10).

 Falling in the tackle:
1. Go down on your knees as if you were going to make a roll.
2. Fall sideways, landing on your hip.
3. Continue to fall letting your shoulder hit the ground.
4. Hold the ball out ready for your teammates to collect.

GO FOR IT!

**When you are
being tackled, try to fall
with your body between the
ball and the player tackling
you. This will give your team
a better chance of
keeping possession.**

- Stay on your feet as long as possible.
- As you fall, roll on to the ground first rolling on to your knees, then your hip, and then your shoulder.

DID YOU KNOW?

The first rugby balls were handmade using leather panels stitched around an inflated pig's bladder. It was the pig's bladder that gave the rugby ball its distinctive shape. The bladder was inflated solely through lung power, by inserting the stem of a clay pipe into the ball and blowing into it.
Early rugby balls varied in size. It was not until 1892 that the actual dimensions of the ball were decided upon and became part of the rules.

- Tuck your shoulder under and roll on to your upper back.

MAKING THE TACKLE

If you go into a tackle half heartedly it could mean that you are not in the correct position and you could get hurt, so it is important to start by practising tackling in stages. You need to be confident that you have mastered each stage before you progress to the next one (see photos opposite):

Stage 1

Start on your knees, with the ball carrier you are tackling on his knees as well.

Stage 2

The ball carrier holds the ball in both arms. Remember, he should not put his arm out to stop himself hitting the ground. Instead, he should roll on to the ground on to his hip and then shoulder.

Stage 3

Once you are comfortable with the technique, get the ball carrier you are tackling to 'walk' slowly past you, with both of you still on your knees.

Tackling stage 1: Get a partner and face each other on your knees.

Stage 2: Go for the tackle.

Stage 3: Down on the ground. Now repeat stages 1 and 2 while 'walking' on your knees.

Stage 4: Practise tackling from a crouch position.

Stage 5: Increase the pace with the ball carrier jogging.

Stage 4

Once you are comfortable with stages 1 to 3, have the ball carrier stand and walk past you while you are in a crouch position, ready to make the tackle.

Stage 5

Then have the ball carrier jog past you while you crouch and make the tackle.

Stage 6

When you are feeling confident, try it with both of you jogging.

Putting it all together

Make sure you have the correct technique at each stage before moving on. When you are ready you can try different types of tackle. There are three main types:

1 The side tackle
2 The front tackle
3 The rear tackle.

To practise the tackles you will need:

- A partner who is roughly the same size and weight as you.
- A rugby ball.
- A soft area to work on, such as grass or, if indoors, mats.

THE SIDE TACKLE

This tackle is made when you are running in to tackle the ball carrier from the side. The most important point to remember is to put your head behind the ball carrier and keep it there throughout the tackle – you don't want the ball carrier landing on your head!

Key points

- Make sure you are to the side of the ball carrier.
- As you go to make the tackle make sure your head will go behind the ball carrier – see photo 1.
- Make sure you have a low body position as you near the ball carrier.
- Keeping your eyes open, position your head behind, or to one side of, the ball carrier (cheek-to-cheek).
- Make contact with your shoulder on the ball carrier's thighs.
- Keep your chin up and your back straight.
- Squeeze your arms tight while driving with your legs.
- Roll to finish on top and get back to your feet quickly.

Side tackle: 1. Go in for the tackle making sure your head is behind the ball carrier's back.

2. Keeping a low position, tackle the ball carrier around the thighs.

3. Drive with your legs and roll.

DID YOU KNOW?

Women's rugby is becoming increasingly popular. A women's game was recorded as far back as 1891 in New Zealand and today the English Rugby Football Union (RFU) estimates that women's rugby is played in 80 different countries around the world. Women's International Rugby began in 1982 and women have their own World Cup run in a similar way to the men's competition.

Key points

- Fix your eyes on the hips of the ball carrier.
- Get low with your arms wide and be light on your feet, so that you can move sideways if the ball carrier tries to run around you.
- Go towards the ball carrier, staying low.
- Make contact with your shoulder just below the ball carrier's waist.
- Wrap your arms around the ball carrier's legs and squeeze.
- Drive with your legs to knock the ball carrier over.
- Make sure that you finish with your head on top of the ball carrier.
- Get back on your feet.

THE FRONT TACKLE

This tackle is made when an opposition player is running at you with the ball. It can be the most difficult tackle to make, but if you do it right it is very effective and can often result in your team winning back the ball.

To make it less intimidating, look at the player you are going to tackle. You are only tackling his legs and waist. His top half doesn't actually matter!

GO FOR IT!

After making your tackle, get back to your feet as quickly as possible. You need to pick up the ball and get it to your own teammates before the opposition supporting players arrive.

1

Front tackle: 1. Go in low with your arms wide.

2

2. Put your arms around the ball carrier's legs.

3

3: Squeeze with your arms and drive forwards to take the ball carrier down.

15

Rear tackle: 1. Go in for the tackle slightly to one side.

THE REAR TACKLE

This tackle is made when an opposition player is running away from you with the ball. You need to be quicker than him, which will often be the case when he is carrying the ball.

The key point here is to drive with your shoulder to knock him over. Remember, always finish with your head on top!

2. Make contact at thigh-height with your head to the side.

Key points

- Make sure you are slightly to the side of the ball carrier.
- As you go to make the tackle, make sure your head will go to the side of the ball carrier.
- Make sure you have a low body position as you get near the ball carrier.
- Keeping your eyes open, position your head to one side of the ball carrier (cheek-to-cheek).

3. Drive and twist to bring down the ball carrier.

No you don't: Gloucester's James Simpson-Daniel executes a fine rear tackle to stop Cardiff's Ben Blair in the 2009 EDF Trophy Final at Twickenham.

- Make contact with your shoulder on the ball carrier's thighs.
- Keep your chin up and your back straight.
- Squeeze your arms tight while driving with the legs.

- Twist and drive slightly sideways so that you land on top of the ball carrier, using him as a soft landing pad!
- Roll to finish on top and get back to your feet quickly.

CONTACT

We have looked at ways to avoid a tackle, but sometimes there is no alternative to carrying the ball into contact with the opposition. It is almost always a last resort, because it would normally be better to pass the ball before being tackled. This helps you to make ground and keep the ball away from the opposing team.

As soon as you get into contact you are taking the ball near to your opponents and they may be able to snatch the ball away from you unless you are careful! Therefore, try to keep the ball away from the opposing team as long as possible until your supporting players can arrive and help.

DID YOU KNOW?

The Southern Hemisphere countries of Australia, New Zealand and South Africa have their own equivalent of Europe's Six Nations tournament, called the Tri Nations.

The national teams are often referred to by their nicknames rather than their nationality – the Wallabies (Australia), the All Blacks (New Zealand) and the Springboks (South Africa).

TAKING THE BALL INTO CONTACT

The main thing to remember when taking the ball into contact is that you need to keep your body between the opposing players and the ball.

To help you, imagine the tackler is a small tree. His body is the trunk of the tree and therefore the strongest part; his arms are the branches and still quite a strong part of the tree; his fingers are the twigs and they are definitely the weakest part of the tree!

So which part do you want to run against if you can't get completely around and there is no one to pass to? His hands.

Allowing yourself to be tackled should always be the last resort.

Key points

- Stay light on your feet so that you move the defender to where you want him – not the other way around.
- Try to run to the side of the tackler – aim for the twigs!
- Keep your chin off your chest and your eyes open.
- Adopt a crouched position, ready to drive up into the tackler.
- Take a big, wide powerful step into contact.

- Keep your body between the defender and the ball.
- Keep your spine parallel to the ground and in line with the direction you are aiming for.

GOING TO GROUND

If your supporting players don't arrive quickly enough you may find yourself getting turned around and the opposing players could get their hands on the ball.

If you have no team support, you may have no choice but to go to ground.

To delay this as long as possible you will have to slide down on to the ground. You are creating a "ruck", (see page 21) which means the opposition cannot get the ball easily as they have to step over you to reach it while staying on their feet. If your supporting players arrive in time, they can knock the opposing players back off the ball and so secure possession.

(see page 21)

GO FOR IT!

Practise landing in a tackle so that you are facing your own team with your back towards the opposition. This will help your team keep possession.

Key points

- Avoid putting your arms out to break your fall. Try to land on your backside or back.
- Slide down the tackler to give yourself support.
- Body first, then ball. Do not throw the ball away. Hold it tightly until you are down on the ground.
- Look for support throughout,

and try to pass off the ground if there is a supporting player arriving.

- Place the ball with outstretched arms immediately away from you and towards your arriving teammates.

THE RUCK

A ruck is formed when the ball is on the ground and at least two players are bound together over the top contesting for the ball.

The ball cannot be handled in a ruck – players must try to hook the ball back with their feet so that it can be picked up by another player once it has left the ruck.

To join the ruck you must bind onto a teammate using the whole of your arm and then try to push the opposition off and away from the ball. Make sure you don't step on the player on the ground, rather try to step over him!

In a ruck the ball is on the ground while players push to gain possession.

THE MAUL

A maul is formed when the ball is held and three or more players (at least one from each team) are bound together contesting for the ball.

To join a maul you must bind on to a teammate with your whole arm and then push the opposition back or try to wrestle the ball free so that you can either run on or pass the ball to a teammate.

DID YOU KNOW?

The Rugby World Cup is controlled by the International Rugby Board (IRB), which was founded in 1886. It governs the sport worldwide and publishes the game's laws and rankings. According to the IRB, rugby is played in more than 100 countries worldwide.

It's tough in there: France's forwards drive for the line in a match against Argentina in the 2007 World Cup.

In a maul you have to wrestle with the other players to get the ball to pass on to a teammate.

TEAMWORK

When a group of players stop playing as individuals and work together to achieve a common goal, we call it teamwork. It is perhaps one of the hardest things to learn as a young player. It is easy to get the ball and run like mad until you are tackled, but, if you had slowed up a bit just before you were tackled, would that have enabled you to pass the ball to a teammate and so keep moving forwards?

You may be a wonderful rugby player, but you are unlikely to defeat an opposing team on your own. It is only by working together that you will be able to perform well and win the game.

WHAT IS GOOD TEAMWORK?

Here are some of the key things that make up good teamwork:

Communication

All members of the team should talk to one another and know what is happening around them. Players should call for the ball and communicate in defence so that there are no gaps left for the opposition to run through.

Encouragement

A good team will be full of players who encourage and support each other even when mistakes are made. No one moans or tells another player off. Only positive comments should be made.

Commitment

All members of the team work hard for each other. No one lets anyone down by not trying. Every individual player makes sure that he does his job and then looks for more to do. Everyone on the team is working towards the same goal.

Respect

All members of the team respect each other and make the effort to listen when someone has something to say.

Roles

Every player in the team knows what his role/position is and what he should do in most situations.

The ability to work as part of a team can make a big difference to how well you perform on the pitch.

LEADERSHIP

Each team needs leaders who will help guide other players towards the right decisions, enabling the team to perform at its best.

Developing leaders within the team

One way of developing leaders is to let players take responsibility for things the team does in training. Ask your coach if you or another player can lead the rest of the team in the warm up at the beginning of the next practice. You could all take turns leading five minutes of the warm up each week until players get used to taking responsibility within the team.

If the coach is agrees he may let players take control of part of the training as well, and in this way close teamwork and trust can be developed throughout the team. It is very important that the team has players who can make decisions on the field during games and help others on the team to follow those decisions. It is no use asking the coach to make the decisions. By the time they have told the team what to do from the touchline the opportunity will have passed!

Leaders

Normally, but not always, the team leaders are those that play in the spine (or backbone) of the team. This means that they are in positions which are central and therefore they can easily see and influence what is happening on the pitch.

A good captain may play on the wing and that is fine, but he will need to be able to communicate and trust players in the spine of the team to enable the team's tactics to be followed.

THE SPINE OF THE TEAM

- Hooker (no. 2)
- Number Eight (no. 8)
- Scrum Half (no. 9)
- Fly Half (no. 10)
- Fullback (no. 15)

If you look at the diagram of the team you will see why these positions are sometimes called the spine. The captain and vice captain of the team are often in one of these positions.

As players grow older, they not only grow physically, but they may also gain in confidence. This

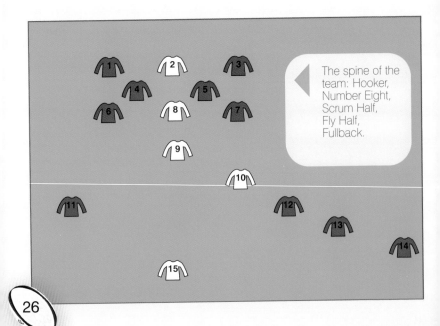

The spine of the team: Hooker, Number Eight, Scrum Half, Fly Half, Fullback.

means that a team's leaders may change from year to year and this is in itself a good thing, as the more players that have a chance to develop as leaders, the better.

The team's leaders help get everyone pulling in the same direction once the game has started, but everyone should have a good idea what tactics the team is going to use to try to win the game. Usually, the team's coach will help players decide what type of game is best suited for what the team is trying to achieve. This is called having a game plan.

DID YOU KNOW?

In the 2003 World Cup Australia scored a record-breaking number of tries in their match against Namibia. The 22 tries contributed to a phenomenal final score of 142-0.

Every team needs a leader who can make decisons quickly during a game.

TACTICS

There are a number of different ways to play the game and each team will try to out-think the other by playing to their own strengths and attempting to exploit the opposition's weaknesses.

For instance, if your team has a very good kicker as fly-half you may plan on a kicking game in your own half. This means that when the play is at your end of the field you work to get the ball to your fly half and rely on him kicking the ball deep into the opposition's half. The key will be to make sure that your players chase up quickly to force the opposition either to kick it back or to get tackled and give you a chance to win the ball back.

However, if the opposition knows that you have a fly half who is a good kicker, they might leave some of their players (their full back and perhaps wingers) deep, waiting for a kick. In that case you could run the ball and catch them unawares!

There are some basic principles of play in rugby that help us to decide which tactics to use.

PRINCIPLES OF PLAY

In rugby the rules that tell everyone how to play the game are known as laws. There are two very strange laws that make the game different from any other. The first is that you have to pass the ball backwards. If you think about it for a moment, what does this actually mean?

In other games, such as football or basketball, if you have the ball you usually pass it to your teammates in the direction you want to go to score (see diagram opposite). In rugby if we pass the ball backwards it means one of the players who has the ball has to run forwards with it, otherwise the team will end up back on its own line. It is this simple law that makes rugby a running game.

The second strange law that makes rugby very different is that once you have scored your team get the ball back!

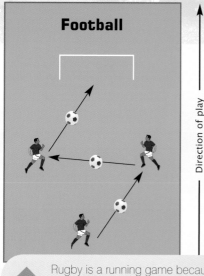

Football

Rugby

Direction of play

 Rugby is a running game because the rules of the game state the ball has to be passed backwards.

Think about it – in football or basketball once you score the other team get the ball to re-start play. In rugby, the opposition have to kick it back to you. If you win the toss at the beginning of the game, you should try to keep the ball and score. Then the other team will kick it back to you, and then you can try to score again, and so on.

This usually doesn't happen, because the team with the ball will eventually make a mistake and so lose possession.

Here are some common mistakes which mean your team will lose possession of the ball:

1. Passing the ball to a member of the opposition team (an interception).

Rugby is unique as the ball has to be passed backwards, and not in the direction of play.

2. Dropping the ball and the opposition team pick it up (losing possession).
3. Passing the ball so that it goes forward (forward pass). The opposition get to put the ball into their own scrum.
4. Kicking the ball to the opposition team.
5. Running or passing the ball into touch (the side of the pitch). The opposition gets to throw the ball into a line out.
6. Committing an offence so that the opposition team is awarded a penalty (and the ball).

GAME PLANS

A team's game plan will constantly be changing as players get better at certain skills, or other circumstances change. But, simply put, the key to winning games is to enable the team to:

BE THE BEST

These are the five "principles of play" in rugby. If you understand them and remember them, it will help you be a better team player!

Name	What it means
Contest possession	Your team try to get the ball.
Go forward	You or a teammate with the ball run forwards with it.
Support	Teammates run near the ball carrier to get a backwards pass from him/her.
Continuity	Teammates keep passing and running forward without losing the ball.
Pressure	The opposing team run out of defenders and you score!

- Keep the ball as much as possible when they have possession.
- When the opposition has the ball, force them to make mistakes and therefore give the ball back.

The game plan will depend on the team's abilities and characteristics, which might include:
- Fast running backs.
- A tall set of forwards.

With these strengths the game plan could be to play a wide running or kicking game, and if the ball goes into touch, there will be a good chance of winning it again in the line out.

Players will need to react to what they see in front of them. If you have the ball and the defenders are spread out wide in front it will be a good idea to attack up the middle (see diagram 1). If the defence are bunched up then attack out wide (see diagram 2).

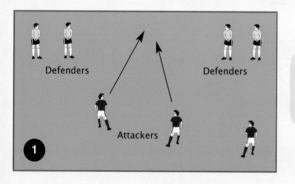

Defenders

Defenders

Attackers

1

If the defence are spread out wide, it may be best to attack up the middle.

If you have a solid line of defence in front of you, your best option may be to attack out wide

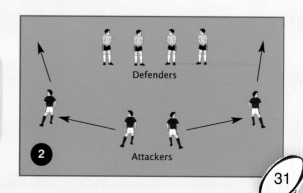

Defenders

Attackers

2

THE LAST **WORD**

Rugby is a fantastic game to play, because it requires a combination of individual skills and teamwork. As you grow older you will find that being a part of a rugby club is a great way to make new friends.

Even if you don't make it to the top, you will still have fun playing rugby for many years. So practise these skills regularly to ensure that you will be the best you can be.

First published 2009 by
A & C Black Publishers Ltd
36 Soho Square, London W1D 3QY
www.acblack.com

Copyright © 2009 Westline Publishing

ISBN: 978-1-4081-1411-7

All rights reserved. No part of this publication may be reproduced in any form or by any means – graphic, electronic or mechanical, including photocopying, recording, taping or information storage and retrieval systems – without the prior permission in writing of the publishers.

The right of Westline Publishing to be identified as the author of this work has been asserted by them in accordance with the Copyright, Designs and Patents Act 1988

Note: It is always the responsibility of the individual to assess his or her own fitness capability before participating in any training activity. Whilst every effort has been made to ensure the content of this book is as technically accurate as possible, neither the author nor the publishers can accept responsibility for any injury or loss sustained as a result of the use of this material.

A CIP catalogue record for this book is available from the British Library.

Text and cover design by Westline Publishing Ltd

Photography: PA Photos (incl. Cover), istockphoto.com and Julia Barnes.

Special thanks to: Issy Johns-Turner, Rebecca Thompson, Yaz Dell, Toby Webb, Carl Manley, Tom Watts, Kane Frith, Charlie Gwyther, Ross Horman and Ben Hobbs.

This book is produced using paper that is made from wood grown in managed, sustainable forests. It is natural, renewable and recyclable. The logging and manufacturing processes conform to the environmental regulations of the country of origin.

Typeset in the UK

Printed and bound in Singapore by Tien Wah Press.

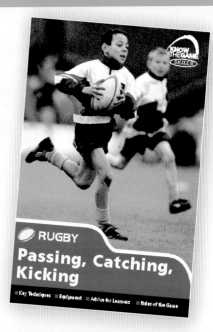

RUGBY
Passing, Catching, Kicking

■ Key Techniques   ■ Equipment   ■ Advice for Learners   ■ Rules of the Game

If you enjoyed this book, you should also read its companion volume, *Rugby: Passing, Catching, Kicking*, available from all good book shops, priced £4.99.

A NOTE ON GENDER
Although the 'he' pronoun is used throughout this book, no gender bias is intended.